I0453709

THE MOURNING AFTER

A RAW AND HONEST GUIDE FOR ANYONE GRIEVING

SHAYNE O'BRIEN

Dedicated to my fellow mourners.

CONTENTS

INTRODUCTION

"How lucky I am to have something that makes saying goodbye so hard." — A.A. Milne

My mother died on a September day in 2017, and as it is with loss, lots of calendar milestones are tough. Yet as difficult as birthdays and anniversaries and holidays are, those are predictable trials. You sort of see those breakdowns coming and you prepare for them. In fact, people are usually much more sensitive to your grief during those times; much more mindful of what might be going on beneath the surface. Your discomfort then seems expected, called for, natural in their eyes.

The really horrible moments are those *other* ones; the random, unexpected, unspectacular times when the pain comes out of nowhere and throat punches your soul. It might be a song or a word or a time of day or the smell of something on the stove or a place you drive past that rips you open again and brings the flood of tears and sobs.

And during many such times it just isn't convenient or socially acceptable to flat-out lose it; at the school with your son or in a staff meeting or paying at the drive-thru or in the middle of a board game with a group of friends. On so many of those occasions, to save yourself the embarrassment or to prevent an awkward moment for those you are with, you grit your teeth, ball up your fist, force a smile and force the tears back down from where they came. You fall apart in places no one can see, and all the while you look perfectly fine.

I've grown to accept that so much of grief is destined to be a solitary road. Even when well-meaning people care deeply and truly desire to share the journey with you, they will never be privy to the frequency and severity of your suffering. This is partly because your loss is so very individual, and partly because you simply never reveal it all to them. You couldn't possibly.

I would have preferred to never have had to walk this road at all. Traveling through the Grief Valley has largely been a big slice of Hell, but it certainly hasn't been without its hard-earned treasures too. One of those has been the realization of just how much hidden pain there is in my midst, of how many of people I cross paths with on any given day might be smiling and silently falling apart.

That kind of awareness doesn't come until

you too have many moments of deeply buried hurt, but once you experience it, you see people differently. You look more intently past the forced smile. Empathy becomes easier. Compassion surfaces involuntarily.

I started writing about grief not because I had studied it, but because I was forced to live it. When you lose someone you love, the world doesn't stop spinning, but *your* world does. And that's where the struggle begins, figuring out how to keep moving forward when everything feels upside down.

If you're reading this, chances are you're hurting. Maybe you just lost someone, or maybe it's been a while, but the ache still lingers. People mean well, but they don't always know what to say. And honestly, most of the time, words don't fix grief. But what I've learned is that small moments of understanding, knowing you're not crazy, not alone, and not doing this "wrong", can make all the difference.

This book isn't a step-by-step plan to get over loss. That's not how grief works. There's no finish line, no deadline, no magic words that make it better. But what I can offer is a companion on the journey. Someone who has walked this road and knows how unpredictable, exhausting, and isolating it can be. I want to give you real, practical help, not platitudes, not clichés, just honest reflections from someone who understands.

The stories at the beginning of each chapter

are based on true experiences, some from friends, others from family members, acquaintances, and even strangers whose paths have crossed mine. In some cases, we've shared long conversations. In others, just a few minutes and a glimpse into their grief story. Names and identifying details have been changed, but the emotions are real. It has been a privilege to walk with each of them, even briefly, in the sacred space of their sorrow.

Wherever you are in your grief, I hope you find something here that helps. And if nothing else, I hope you find permission to grieve in your own way, in your own time.

To all those who will willingly suffer in secret today, as memories and sadness surprise you in the most inconvenient of moments: I see you. I know your pain doesn't have to be visible to be real. That's what this guide is for.

Take a deep breath. You're not alone.

Let's get started.

1

THE UNEXPECTED LANDMINES OF GRIEF

"Grief is like the ocean; it comes in waves, ebbing and flowing. Sometimes the water is calm, and sometimes it is overwhelming. All we can do is learn to swim." — Vicki Harrison

Martha had been doing okay—or at least she thought she was. It had been six months since her husband, Tom, passed away, and she had learned how to go through the motions of daily life. She went to work, paid the bills, and even managed to meet a friend for coffee now and then. But one afternoon, while walking through the grocery store, she turned down the coffee aisle and saw his favorite brand sitting on the shelf. Without warning, a wave of grief crashed over her. Her breath caught in her throat, and she felt the sting of tears in her eyes.

She reached out instinctively, as if she might still buy it for him, before realizing—again—that he was gone. The world around her continued as normal, shoppers passing by, carts squeaking against the floor. But in that moment, in the middle of the store, her loss felt as fresh as the day he died.

She left her cart in the aisle and walked straight to her car, then sat in the parking lot with her hands gripping the steering wheel. The tears came in heavy sobs, and she let them. She hadn't expected this moment, but here it was. A grief ambush. And all she could do was ride the wave.

Grief doesn't run on a schedule. It doesn't follow a neat, predictable pattern. Instead, it sneaks up on you in the middle of an ordinary day, when you least expect it.

Maybe it's a smell, the cologne they wore or the scent of their favorite meal cooking in a restaurant. Maybe it's a song that plays while you're waiting in line at the grocery store, or a phrase someone says that instantly transports you back to a moment when they were still here. Whatever it is, grief has a way of blindsiding you, making even the simplest moments feel impossibly heavy.

I call these "grief landmines." They're scattered all over the landscape of your life, and you don't always know where they are until you step on one. And when you do, it feels like you're right back at day one—like no time has passed, like the loss is fresh all over again.

It's frustrating. It's exhausting. And it's completely normal.

Most people think of grief as something that hits hardest on the "big" days—holidays, birthdays, anniversaries. And while those days can be difficult, sometimes it's the smallest, most unexpected moments that hurt the most. A sunny Saturday morning. A drive past their favorite coffee shop. The silence of an empty chair at the table.

The problem is, the world around you doesn't see these landmines. Other people aren't feeling what you're feeling, which can make grief incredibly isolating. You might be holding it together on the outside, going through the motions, but inside, you're still bleeding.

So what do you do?

First, recognize that these moments are going to happen. You can't prevent them, but you can remind yourself that they're normal. Grief isn't a straight line; it's a series of waves, and some days, those waves hit harder than others.

Second, give yourself permission to feel it. There's nothing wrong with being fine one moment and a mess the next. You don't have to justify your grief to anyone, not even yourself.

And finally, be kind to yourself in those moments. Take a breath. Step away if you need to. Find something that helps you ground yourself—

a walk, a song that soothes rather than stings, a deep breath, a call to a friend who understands.

Grief doesn't mean you're broken. It means you loved someone deeply. And when you love someone deeply, their absence leaves a mark.

If you're feeling like grief keeps ambushing you, you're not alone. And you're not doing this wrong. You're just grieving.

And that's okay.

WHAT AM I FEELING RIGHT NOW?

One Step to Take

When a grief landmine hits, take a deep breath and name what you're feeling. Say it out loud or write it down: "This moment just reminded me of them, and it hurts." Giving words to your emotions can help ground you.

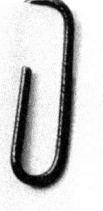

Remember!

"Grief landmines are part of the story. You're not broken, they just hit hard."

2

THE THINGS PEOPLE SAY

❝ *"No one ever told me that grief felt so like fear."*
    — C.S. Lewis

aniel stood at the door of the church, shaking hands and exchanging nods with people who had come to pay their respects to his father. He had barely registered most of the conversations, just a blur of kind words, quiet condolences, and pats on the shoulder.

Then, an old friend of his father's clasped his arm and said, "You've got to be strong for your mother now."

Daniel felt a lump rise in his throat. What he wanted to say was, "I'm grieving too." He wanted to tell the man that he hadn't slept in days, that he'd just held his father's hand while he took his last breath, and now, here he was, expected to step into the role of the strong one, as if his own grief didn't exist.

Daniel nodded politely in an effort not to make the moment any more painful. The line of mourners continued. But inside, Daniel felt smaller, like his grief had been quietly placed on a shelf while the room moved on.

When People Say the Wrong Thing

One of the hardest parts of grief is hearing well-meaning but painful words from others. People don't mean to be hurtful. They just don't know what to say. They try to comfort, but their words often miss the mark.

You might hear things like:

- *"They're in a better place."* Maybe that's true, but as the grieving person, the best place for my loved one was here. This only makes loss feel minimized.
- *"Everything happens for a reason."* Grief doesn't feel reasonable. Hearing this can make you feel like you need to figure out some grand purpose for your pain when all you really need is space to hurt.

- *"I know how you feel."* Even if you've lost someone, grief is personal. No two losses are the same. You need someone to acknowledge your pain and listen.
- *"God needed another angel."* Even if you believe in heaven, this can make it sound like your loss was intentional, like your loved one was taken for a divine reason. That's hard to hear when you are in pain.
- *"Call me if you need anything."* This comes from a good place, but most of us who are grieving don't even know what we need. And we are not going call. It can end up feeling like the support is on hold, waiting for *me* to activate it, as if now it's my job to reach out when I'm the one barely holding it together.

Even if these words are meant to bring comfort, they can feel dismissive. They don't acknowledge the depth of your pain. They may even make you feel like you should be "handling this better."

What to Do When Words Hurt

1. **Recognize That Most People Mean Well.** It's frustrating when

someone says something that stings, but remembering that they *mean* to be supportive, however clumsy their words, can take the edge off the hurt. Most people are simply uncomfortable with grief and say things to try to fix or soften it. That doesn't mean you have to like what they say, but it may help to recognize that their words are more about *their discomfort* than your grief.

2. **You Don't Have to Respond Right Away.** If someone says something that upsets you, it's okay to take a breath and not respond immediately. You don't owe anyone a perfect reaction. You can simply nod, say *"Thanks for checking in"* or *"I appreciate you being here."* Not every comment requires a response.

3. **Give Yourself Permission to Feel Annoyed or Hurt.** It's okay if certain phrases bother you. It's okay to feel misunderstood. You don't have to dismiss your own feelings just because someone else meant well.

4. **Set Boundaries When Needed.** If someone repeatedly

says things that minimize your grief, it's okay to set a boundary. You can gently say, *"I know you're trying to help, but that's not what I need right now."* Or, *"I just need someone to listen."* It's not your job to educate everyone, but you can advocate for yourself.

5. **Find a Safe Place to Express Your Feelings.** Sometimes, the best thing you can do is process frustrating comments with someone who understands, whether it's a friend, a grief group, or a journal entry. Venting in a safe space can help you let go of the frustration instead of letting it build up.

WHAT AM I FEELING RIGHT NOW?

One Step to Take

Give yourself permission to set boundaries. If someone says something hurtful, it's okay to respond with, "Thank you. I know you mean well and want to help." If you feel you can it's ok to add, "I'm just not sure that's what I need right now."

Remember!

"Sometimes the things people say make it worse. You're not overreacting. You're grieving."

3
WHEN THE FUNERAL IS OVER

"When someone you love dies, you never quite get over it. You just slowly learn how to go on without them. But always keeping them tucked safely in your heart." — Unknown

Sophia had spent the past two weeks in a whirlwind—making funeral arrangements, sorting through paperwork, and accepting a steady stream of condolences. People had surrounded her in the beginning. Her fridge was packed with casseroles, and her phone had constantly buzzed with messages from friends checking in. She had barely had a moment to think.

But now, the house was quiet. Too quiet.

This morning, for the first time in weeks, no one had called. No one had stopped by. She sat at the kitchen table, staring at the empty seat where *her husband, James, used to sit. She had grown so accustomed to people filling the space that she hadn't considered what it would feel like when they stopped.*

Sophia reached for her phone, scrolling through her messages. The texts had slowed. The calls had nearly stopped. Life was moving forward for everyone else, but for her, time felt frozen. She hesitated, then typed out a message to her friend, Emily: "Hey, I know everyone is busy, but today has been really hard. Would you have time for coffee?"

She hovered over the send button. Would she sound needy? Would Emily think she should be further along in her grief? She nearly deleted it—but instead, she took a deep breath and hit send.

Within seconds, she could see Emily was responding. "Of course. I'll be there in 20 minutes." Sophia exhaled, for the first time in a few days she didn't feel completely invisible.

The funeral is over. The flowers have wilted. The cards stop coming. And suddenly, the world expects you to "move on." But the truth is, this is when grief often hits the hardest.

In the days immediately after a loss, people show up. They bring meals, send messages, and check in. But as time passes, life goes back to normal, for everyone else. For you, though, normal is gone. And that's when grief can feel incredibly lonely.

This is the time when you need support the most. Not in the rush of the funeral, but in the quiet that follows. It's in the everyday moments— the empty chair at dinner, the phone that doesn't ring, the routines that now feel hollow.

If you're feeling like people have forgotten, they haven't, they just don't realize how long grief lasts. It's okay to remind them. It's okay to ask for support. And it's okay to still be grieving, long after the funeral is over.

Take your time. Grief doesn't have a deadline. You are allowed to heal at your own pace. Some days will be harder than others, and that's okay.

Healing isn't about forgetting—it's about learning how to carry the love forward, even as you carry the loss.

WHAT AM I FEELING RIGHT NOW?

One Step to Take

Make a list of two or three people who truly care about you. Send one of them a text or call them. Let them know you're struggling. Connection doesn't have to be big—it just has to be intentional.

Remember!

"You're not failing at grief because you still hurt. This is what mourning looks like."

4

THE WEIGHT OF GRIEF – EMOTIONAL AND PHYSICAL EXHAUSTION

"Grief and love are conjoined—you don't get one without the other." — Jandy Nelson

Jordan had always been the reliable one. The one people leaned on. When his sister passed away unexpectedly, he was the one making arrangements, comforting his parents, and handling the never-ending logistics that came with loss. It had been months now, and the world had gone back to normal, at least for everyone else.

But Jordan felt different. He was exhausted all the time. His body ached, his head was constantly foggy, and even the smallest tasks felt overwhelming. He had never struggled to get out of bed before, but now, some mornings, it felt like a monumental effort just to put his feet on the floor.

One afternoon, he met up with his old high school friend, Caleb, who had lost his father a few *years back. They sat across from each other at their favorite diner, the silence between them more comfortable than words. After a while, Jordan sighed and muttered, "I don't know what's wrong with me. I feel like I should be doing better by now, but I'm just so tired all the time."*

Caleb set his coffee down and leaned in. "That's grief, man. It's heavy. No one tells you how much it takes out of you, physically, mentally, everything. When my dad passed, I kept pushing through like nothing had changed, and my body shut down on me. I didn't sleep, didn't eat right, just kept going until I couldn't anymore. You can't do that. You've got to rest."

Jordan stared at the table, his fingers tracing the rim of his mug. He hadn't thought about it that way. He'd just assumed he was failing at handling things. "How did you get through it?"

Caleb shrugged. "I stopped pretending I was fine. I let myself slow down. I took breaks when I needed them. And I stopped feeling guilty about it. You don't have to power through this, Jordan. You need to give yourself the same care you'd give anyone else going through this."

For the first time Jordan felt like someone understood. Maybe he wasn't weak, he was just grieving.

Grief isn't just emotional, it's physical. It seeps into your body, making even the simplest tasks feel like climbing a mountain. You may feel tired all the time, yet unable to sleep. You might find yourself forgetting things, struggling to focus, or feeling like you're moving in slow motion. This isn't just in your head, it's grief taking a toll on your body.

Why Does Grief Make You So Tired?

Grief is work. It takes an enormous amount of mental and emotional energy to process loss. Your brain is constantly adjusting to a new reality, one where someone who was once a part of your life is no longer here. That kind of adjustment is exhausting. Add in the stress, sadness, and sometimes anxiety or regret, and it's no wonder your body feels worn out.

When you're grieving, your brain and body are working overtime. Your nervous system is often on high alert, cycling through emotions like sadness, anger, disbelief, and deep longing. All of this takes energy, leaving you drained before the day even begins.

Recognizing the Physical Symptoms of Grief

Everyone experiences grief differently, but common physical symptoms include:

- **Extreme fatigue** – Feeling exhausted even after a full night's sleep.
- **Changes in appetite** – Some people lose their appetite entirely, while others find themselves eating more for comfort.
- **Sleep disturbances** – Struggling to fall asleep, waking up frequently, or sleeping more than usual.
- **Body aches and tension** – Grief can manifest as headaches, back pain, or tightness in the chest.
- **Brain fog** – Difficulty concentrating, forgetfulness, or feeling mentally "foggy."

How to Cope with the Exhaustion of Grief

1. **Give Yourself Permission to Rest.** Your body is carrying a heavy load. Don't expect yourself to function at full capacity. If you need more sleep, take it. If you need quiet, seek it. Rest is not laziness, it's healing.

2. **Eat, Even When You Don't Feel Like It.** Grief can mess with your appetite, but your body still

needs fuel. Try to eat small, healthy meals, even if you don't feel hungry. Your energy levels depend on it.

3. **Move, Even a Little.** Exercise might be the last thing on your mind, but movement can help. A short walk, stretching, or deep breathing exercises can reduce tension and help your body process stress.

4. **Lower Your Expectations.** This is not the time to push yourself to be highly productive. If all you did today was get out of bed and breathe, that's enough. Let go of unnecessary pressures and focus on what truly matters.

5. **Create Small Routines.** When everything feels overwhelming, simple routines can provide stability. Whether it's making a cup of tea in the morning or taking a short walk each evening, small habits can help ground you.

6. **Talk About It.** Holding grief inside can make it feel even heavier. Whether it's with a trusted friend, a support group, or a counselor, sharing

your emotions can help lighten the burden.

7. **Be Patient with Yourself.** Grief doesn't run on a schedule, and neither does your energy level. Some days will be better than others. Allow yourself to move at your own pace without guilt.

WHAT AM I FEELING RIGHT NOW?

One Step to Take

Pick one small act of self-care today: drink a glass of water, stretch for a minute, or step outside for fresh air. Tiny moments of care add up.

Remember!

"Grief doesn't just hurt your heart, it drains your energy. You're not lazy. You're human."

5
COPING WITH THE LONELINESS OF GRIEF

"The reality is that you will grieve forever. You will not 'get over' the loss of a loved one; you will learn to live with it." — Elisabeth Kübler-Ross

Marcus never thought he'd be the one to get the call. His younger brother, Devin, had been in a car accident, gone in an instant. No warning. No last words. Just here one moment and gone the next. It didn't feel real, not at the funeral, not when he signed the paperwork, not when people told him, "If you need anything, let me know."

But now, two months later, it felt real. Too real.

The silence in his apartment was unbearable. He had lived alone for years, but this kind of quiet was different. Before, Devin would text him funny memes every night or call just to talk about noth-

ing. Now, Marcus would check his phone and see nothing but empty notifications. He used to love his solitude, but now it felt suffocating.

Tonight, he tried something different. He grabbed his keys and walked to the bar down the street, just to be around people. Not to talk, not to make friends, just to not be alone with his thoughts. He sat at the counter, ordered a drink, and scrolled mindlessly through his phone. No one noticed him, and for once, that was exactly what he wanted.

He wasn't okay. He wasn't sure when he would be. But for tonight, he wasn't alone.

One of the hardest parts of grief isn't just the sadness, it's the loneliness. When you lose someone you love, you don't just miss them; you also lose the routines, conversations, and presence that made up your daily life. It can feel like there's an empty space that no one else can fill.

Why Grief Feels So Lonely

1. **People Move On Faster Than You Do.** In the early days of loss, there's often a flood of support. Friends and family check in, people send messages, and you feel surrounded. But as weeks turn into months, that support often fades. Not

because people don't care, but because life keeps moving for them, even if it feels frozen for you.

2. **Your World Has Changed—Theirs Hasn't.** When you lose someone close to you, everything shifts. You see the world differently. Certain places, songs, or traditions may now feel painful. But for most people around you, life looks the same. That disconnect can make you feel isolated, like you're living in a different reality than everyone else.

3. **Grief Is Personal.** Even if others have experienced loss, no two grief journeys are the same. Your relationship with the person you lost was unique, which means your grief is unique too. That can make it hard to find people who truly understand what you're going through.

How to Cope with the Loneliness of Grief

1. **Acknowledge the Loneliness.** It's okay to admit that you feel alone. Grief is already exhausting, and trying to pretend you're fine when

you're not can make it worse. Recognizing your loneliness doesn't mean you're weak, it means you're human.

2. **Reach Out to Someone You Trust.** Sometimes, people want to help but don't know how. If you're feeling isolated, don't be afraid to send a message or ask a friend to meet for coffee. The people who truly care about you will be glad to hear from you.

3. **Find a Support Group.** Whether in-person or online, grief support groups can be incredibly helpful. Being around others who "get it" can ease some of the isolation. If you're not comfortable talking in a group, even just listening to others share their stories can help.

4. **Talk About the Person You Lost.** One of the most painful parts of grief is feeling like your loved one is disappearing from conversation. It's okay to bring up their name, share stories, or celebrate their memory. The people who love you will listen.

5. **Allow Yourself to Grieve in Your Own Way.** Loneliness doesn't mean you're doing grief wrong. Some people find comfort in being around others, while others need more quiet time alone. There's no "right" way to handle grief. Do what feels right for you.

6. **Take Small Steps Toward Connection.** Loneliness can make you want to withdraw even more. Try to push back against that instinct by taking small steps, sending a text, going for a walk with a friend, or even just sitting in a public place where you're around others.

WHAT AM I FEELING RIGHT NOW?

One Step to Take

Look for a small way to break the cycle of isolation today. It could be sending a text, joining an online grief support group, or even sitting in a café just to be around people. Connection starts with small steps.

Remember!

"Sometimes the quiet is the loudest part of grief."

6

GRIEVING WHILE TAKING CARE OF OTHERS

> "Taking care of yourself doesn't mean me first; it means me too." — L.R. Knost

Rachel stared at the stack of laundry on the couch, the dishes in the sink, and the unread emails piling up on her phone. She had been running on autopilot since losing her baby at sixteen weeks pregnant. There was no funeral, no ceremony, just a quiet, devastating loss that most people seemed to move past much faster than she could.

But Rachel didn't have time to fall apart. She had a three-year-old who still needed bedtime stories and a husband who still needed his best friend. She had responsibilities, and grief wasn't an excuse to let everything go. At least, that's what she told herself.

Tonight, after putting her daughter to bed, Rachel sat on the bathroom floor, the cool tile pressing against her legs. She had been so busy making sure everyone else was okay that she hadn't let herself stop, not once. She covered her face with her hands, the weight of everything finally pressing down.

A soft knock on the door pulled her out of the moment. Her husband, Nate, peeked his head in. "Hey," he said gently. "You don't have to do everything. You know that, right?"

Rachel wanted to argue, to say she was fine. Instead, she just shook her head. Because she wasn't.

Nate sat beside her, not saying anything. Just being there.

And for the first time since the miscarriage, Rachel let herself lean into the silence.

One of the hardest parts of grief is carrying your own pain while still showing up for others. Maybe you're a parent, a spouse, or a caregiver. Maybe people depend on you at work or in your family. Whatever the case, grief doesn't put life on pause, and that can be overwhelming.

Balancing Your Grief and Responsibilities

1. **Give Yourself Grace.** You don't have to be perfect. You don't have to have it all together. If all you can do today is show up and breathe, that's enough.

2. **Set Boundaries.** It's okay to say no. If you're used to taking care of everyone else, grief is a time to recognize that you can't do everything. Give yourself permission to take a step back when needed.

3. **Ask for Help.** You don't have to do this alone. Whether it's asking a friend to pick up groceries, delegating work tasks, or letting family members know you need a break, reach out. People want to help, but they often don't know how unless you tell them.

4. **Find Moments for Yourself.** Even if it's five minutes in the morning with a cup of coffee, a short walk outside, or listening to a favorite song, create space for your grief. Pushing it down doesn't make it go away, it just builds up.

5. **Let Go of Guilt.** If you're grieving while caring for others, you may feel guilty for not being "stronger" or for taking time for yourself. Remember, you can't pour from an empty cup. Taking care of yourself helps you show up better for those who need you.

WHAT AM I FEELING RIGHT NOW?

One Step to Take

Choose one responsibility that you can delegate or take a break from today. Even if it's small, giving yourself a little space can help lighten the load.

Remember!

"Holding it together for others is exhausting. Don't forget to hold space for yourself too."

7
SPECIAL DAYS AND HOLIDAYS WITHOUT THEM

❝ *"Although it's difficult today to see beyond the sorrow, may looking back in memory help comfort you tomorrow."*
— Unknown

David had spent the last twenty years celebrating Christmas with his wife, Julia. Every year, they followed the same traditions, picking out a tree together, watching old holiday movies, making her grandmother's special sugar cookies. This year, none of it felt right.

Julia had battled cancer for three years before passing away in the spring. Now, as December approached, David found himself avoiding the holiday aisle at the store. He hadn't unpacked the decorations, hadn't made plans, hadn't even thought about sending out cards. He wasn't sure he could do Christmas without her.

On Christmas Eve, his daughter called. "Dad, do you want to come over tomorrow? You don't have to, but we'd love to have you."

David hesitated. The thought of sitting in a room full of people, pretending to be okay, felt unbearable. But the idea of spending the day alone wasn't much better. "I don't know," he admitted. "It doesn't feel right without your mom."

His daughter's voice was soft. "I know, Dad. It won't be the same. But we can just be together. No pressure."

That night, David sat in his chair, staring at the box of Christmas decorations in the corner of the room. He wasn't ready to open it. Maybe next year. Maybe never. "I'm going to go", he thought. Not because it would fix anything, but because being alone wouldn't fix it either.

He let out a long breath and whispered, "One step at a time."

Certain days on the calendar hit harder than others. Birthdays, anniversaries, holidays, and other milestones bring fresh waves of grief, often catching you off guard. These days can feel impossible to get through, but with some preparation and grace, you can navigate them in a way that honors both your grief and your love.

Ways to Approach Special Days

1. **Acknowledge the Day.** Trying to ignore a significant day can sometimes make it hurt more. Recognizing that it will be tough allows you to plan ahead and decide what will help you cope.

2. **Decide How You Want to Spend It.** You may want to keep traditions the same, change them, or create new ones. There is no right or wrong way to handle these days— only what feels best for you.

3. **Include Their Memory.** Light a candle, make their favorite meal, share stories, or visit a meaningful place. Finding ways to honor them can make the day feel more connected instead of purely painful.

4. **Give Yourself Permission to Feel.** Whether the day brings tears, laughter, or both, it's all okay. Let yourself experience whatever emotions come up without judgment.

5. **Have a Support System.** Let someone close to you know that the

day is significant. Even if you don't want to be around others, having someone check in on you can be comforting.

6. **Be Flexible.** What works for one year may not work for the next. Give yourself the grace to adjust your plans based on what you need at that moment.

WHAT AM I FEELING RIGHT NOW?

One Step to Take

Make a list of special days and holidays coming up in the next year, anniversaries, birthdays (including your own), Thanksgiving, Christmas, or any date that carries meaning. Once you have your list, spend some time thinking through what you want those days to look like. What have you done in the past? Would it feel comforting to keep that tradition, or would it help to try something new that fits your life now? Having even a simple plan in place can ease the anxiety that often builds as those days approach. Whether big or small, making a plan for the day can offer just a bit more peace when everything feels fragile.

Remember!

"You don't have to pretend the day is normal when everything about it has changed."

8

WHEN GRIEF CHANGES OVER TIME

❝ *"Grief never ends... but it changes. It's a passage, not a place to stay." —* Unknown

Lisa never expected grief to be so unpredictable. When she lost her mother two years ago, she had assumed the pain would follow a straight line, intense at first, but gradually fading over time. And for a while, that seemed to be true. The first year was brutal, but as the months passed, the weight felt a little lighter.

Then, out of nowhere, the grief returned like a punch to the gut.

She had been cleaning out a closet when she found an old sweater, her mother's favorite, still carrying her scent. The moment Lisa held it up, the tears came fast and hard. She sank to the floor, clutching the fabric, the ache as raw as the day she said goodbye.

Later that evening, she sat at her kitchen table, staring at her untouched dinner. She had thought she was "doing better." That's what everyone had told her. But was she? If grief could still hit this hard, did that mean she was going backward?

She picked up her phone and texted her older sister: "Do you ever have days where it feels like Mom just died yesterday?"

The response came almost instantly: "All the time."

Maybe grief didn't follow a straight line. Maybe it looped, circled back, caught you off guard when you least expected it. And maybe that was okay.

Grief doesn't stay the same. It shifts, evolves, and surprises you in ways you don't expect. Some days, it may feel lighter, and then, suddenly, it can come crashing down again. Understanding that grief changes over time can help you navigate the unpredictable waves.

What to Expect as Grief Evolves

1. Grief Comes in Waves

Early on, grief can feel like an overwhelming flood. As time passes, the waves may come less frequently, but when they do hit, they can still be just as intense. That's normal.

2. Moments of Joy Can Feel Strange

At some point, you'll catch yourself laughing or feeling happy, and then you might feel guilty for it. But joy doesn't mean you've forgotten. It means you're learning to carry your grief alongside life.

3. Anniversaries and Milestones Can Stir Up Emotions

Even when you think you're doing okay, certain dates, places, or experiences can bring a rush of emotions. These moments don't mean you're going backward, they're just part of how grief works.

4. Grief Changes, But It Doesn't Disappear

You don't "move on" from grief, but you do learn to live with it differently. The pain might soften, but the love and the loss remain part of you.

How to Navigate Changing Grief

- **Let Yourself Feel What Comes**. There's no timeline for healing, and no "right" way to grieve. If an old memory brings a fresh wave of tears, that's okay. If a good day makes you feel guilty, remind yourself that it's okay to have both grief and joy.
- **Create Space to Remember**. Over time, you may find comfort in keeping certain traditions, creating new ones, or finding quiet ways to honor your loved one.
- **Recognize Growth**. You may not feel it daily, but if you look back, you'll see ways you've adapted, learned, and carried your loved one's memory forward.

WHAT AM I FEELING RIGHT NOW?

One Step to Take

Take a moment to reflect on how your grief has changed over time. Write down one thing that feels different now than it did in the beginning—whether it's harder, easier, or just different.

Remember!

"You're not moving on. You're moving forward—with them in your heart."

9
FINDING PURPOSE
AFTER LOSS

"Tears shed for another person are not a sign of weakness. They are a sign of a pure heart." — José N. Harris

For 53 years, Jerry had built a life with Lucille. They had done everything together, raised kids, traveled, built a home filled with memories. When she was diagnosed with pancreatic cancer, they had four months to say goodbye. It wasn't enough time. It would never have been enough.

Now, the house was just a house. The routines they had built together felt hollow. He found himself making dinners she would like and buying brands that Lucille had always picked. He had built so much of his life around things she loved. Who was he without her?

At first, he drifted. Days blurred together. But

one afternoon, his neighbor, Tom, called. "Hey Jerry, my porch light's out, and I can't figure out what's wrong. Think you could take a look?"

Jerry almost said no. He almost made an excuse. But instead, he grabbed his tools and headed to Tom's house. It took ten minutes to fix, but by the time they were done, Tom patted him on the back. "You're a lifesaver, Jerry. I'd be standing in the dark without you."

The next week, someone at church mentioned their AC was acting up. Jerry knew HVAC, and before he could second-guess himself, he offered to take a look. Then it was a friend's electrical issue. Then a leaky faucet.

Jerry didn't set out to stay busy, he just saw people who needed help. And little by little, helping them brought him some relief and eventually brought him back to life. Not in a grand way, not in a way that erased his grief, but in a way that gave his days some weight, some meaning.

He still misses Lucille every single day. He always will. But he was learning something important, purpose didn't have to be big. Sometimes, it was as simple as fixing a porch light for someone who needed it.

One of the most challenging aspects of grief is figuring out how to live in a world without the person you lost. Over time, you may find yourself asking, "What now?" Finding meaning after loss doesn't mean forgetting, it means learning how to carry love and grief together.

Ways to Find Purpose Again

1. Give Yourself Time

There's no rush to "figure it out." Some people find meaning quickly, while for others, it takes years. Both are okay.

2. Honor Their Memory

Doing something in their honor, volunteering, creating something, or supporting a cause they loved, can be a way to keep their presence alive in your life.

3. Reconnect with What Matters to You

Grief shifts priorities. You may find yourself drawn to things you once loved or exploring new interests. Follow what feels right.

4. Help Others

Sometimes, the most healing thing we can do is support others who are struggling. Sharing your experience or simply being there for someone else can bring unexpected meaning.

5. **Allow Purpose to Be Fluid**

What brings meaning today may change over time. Stay open to growth and new ways of honoring your journey.

WHAT AM I FEELING RIGHT NOW?

One Step to Take

Think of one small way you can lean into your value and purpose today. Maybe it's opening a door for someone, fixing something that's broken, helping a neighbor, painting, planting, or simply sitting with a friend over coffee. It doesn't have to be big to be meaningful. Sometimes showing up for someone else helps you remember that you still matter too.

Remember!

"Sometimes the most healing thing you can do is help someone else with what you've learned to survive."

CONCLUSION: WALKING FORWARD WITH GRIEF

66 *"There is no grief like the grief that does not speak."* — Henry Wadsworth Longfellow

Grief isn't something you get over, it's something you learn to carry. The weight of loss may shift over time, but the love you have for the person who's gone never fades. This journey isn't about forgetting, fixing, or reaching a final destination. It's about finding a way to keep living while holding space for the grief and the love that remain.

You will have hard days. You will have unexpected waves of sadness. And you will also have moments of joy, laughter, and connection again. None of these cancel out the others, they all co-exist as part of your healing.

Wherever you are in this journey, remember: You are not alone. There is no right way to grieve, and there is no timeline you must follow. Be patient with yourself, extend yourself grace, and take things one step at a time.

Grief is the high price we pay for love. And love, in all its forms, is worth carrying forward.

QUOTE SOURCES

The following are the sources for the quotes used throughout this book, shared with deep gratitude to those whose words gave voice to the weight of our grief.

Introduction
"How lucky I am to have something that makes saying goodbye so hard."
—A.A. Milne (attributed; popularized from *Winnie-the-Pooh*)

Chapter 1
"Grief is like the ocean; it comes in waves, ebbing and flowing..."
—Vicki Harrison (widely circulated, exact origin unclear)

Chapter 2
"No one ever told me that grief felt so like fear."
—C.S. Lewis, *A Grief Observed* (1961)

Chapter 3
"When someone you love becomes a memory, the memory becomes a treasure."
—Author unknown

Chapter 4
"Grief and love are conjoined—you don't get one without the other."
—Jandy Nelson, *The Sky Is Everywhere* (2010)
Chapter 5
"The reality is that you will grieve forever... You will learn to live with it."
—Elisabeth Kübler-Ross and David Kessler, *On Grief and Grieving* (2005)
Chapter 6
"Taking care of yourself doesn't mean me first. It means me too."
—L.R. Knost, *Two Thousand Kisses a Day* (2013)
Chapter 7
"Although it's difficult today to see beyond the sorrow, may looking back in memory help comfort you tomorrow."
—Author unknown
Chapter 8
"Grief never ends... but it changes. It's a passage, not a place to stay."
—Author unknown (widely attributed to grief support resources)
Chapter 9
"Tears shed for another person are not a sign of weakness. They are a sign of a pure heart."
—José N. Harris, *MI VIDA: A Story of Faith, Hope and Love* (2010)

Conclusion

"There is no grief like the grief that does not speak."

—Henry Wadsworth Longfellow, *Hyperion: A Romance* (1839)

Copyright © 2025 by Shayne O'Brien

All rights reserved.

No part of this book may be reproduced in any form or by any electronic or mechanical means, including information storage and retrieval systems, without written permission from the author, except for the use of brief quotations in a book review.

www.ingramcontent.com/pod-product-compliance
Lightning Source LLC
Chambersburg PA
CBHW051641120626
46551CB00014B/2172